THE
WHOLEFOOD COOKBOOK

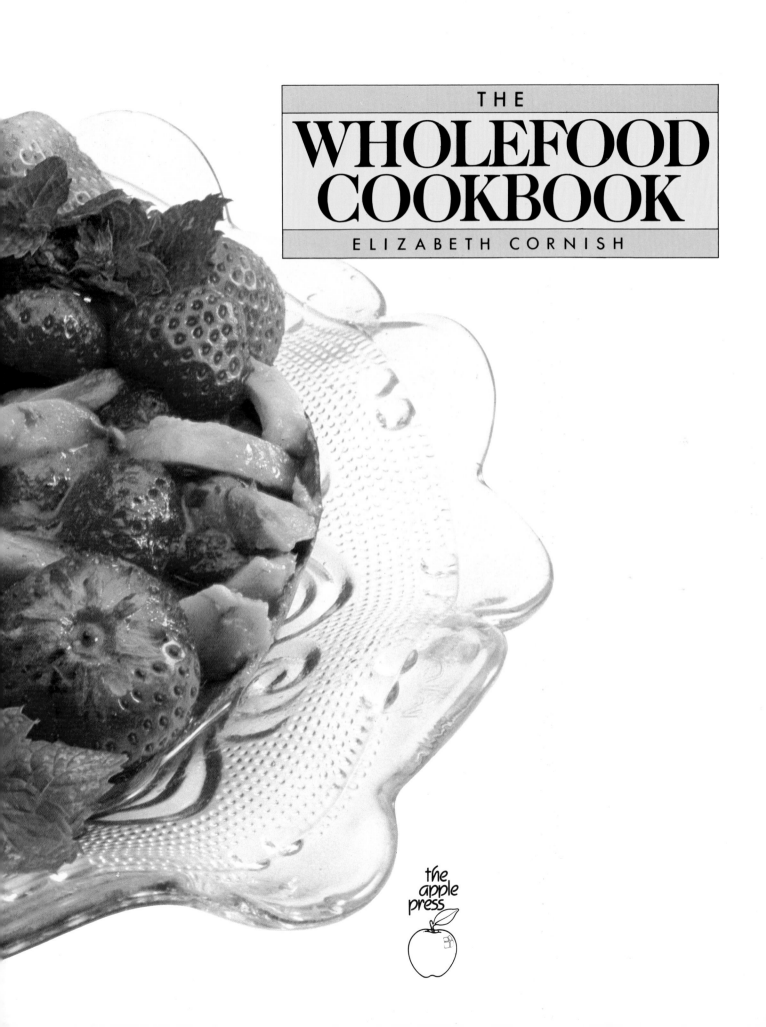

THE

WHOLEFOOD COOKBOOK

ELIZABETH CORNISH

the
apple
press

A QUINTET BOOK

Published by Apple Press Ltd
293 Gray's Inn Road
London WC1X 8QF

ISBN 1 85076 026 8

This book was designed and produced by
Quintet Publishing Limited
6 Blundell Street, London N7

Art design by Bridgewater Associates
Photographer John Heseltine
Illustrator Lorraine Harrison
Editor Cheen Horn

Typeset in Great Britain by
Q.V. Typesetting Limited, London
Colour origination in Hong Kong by
Hong Kong Graphic Arts Company Limited, Hong Kong
Printed in Hong Kong by Leefung-Asco
Printers Limited

C O N T E N T S

The first pleasure of wholefood cookery is the goodness it brings to your table. The freshness and flavour of natural foods, unrefined and free from additives, offers a range of ingredients that is infinitely rich and subtle. But wholefood eating doesn't only satisfy the palate, it brings long-term health benefits too.

Our Western diet tends to be soft, sweet and high in animal fats. Over-refined and processed foods contain fewer vitamins and minerals, and chemical additives can cause unpleasant side effects. The foods closest to nature — fresh fruit and vegetables, unrefined grains, nuts and pulses — are high in vitamins and minerals, high in fibre and low in fat. They provide cheaper protein and satisfy at moderate calorie levels.

So a wholefood diet not only tastes delicious — it offers protection against Western diseases such as heart attacks, obesity, tooth decay and ailments of the lower digestive system.

When the recent interest in healthy eating first sprang up, we were encouraged to chew our way through vast amounts of raw food because it did us good. But wholefood is not medicine. For a modest outlay you can stock your larder with pulses and grains, honey and molasses, fruit and vegetables, and your fridge with fruit juice, cheese and cream cheese. If you are fond of fish and meat, you can treat yourself to a little of these too.

With these delicious natural ingredients at hand you have all you need to create and enjoy a mouthwateringly varied and nutritious cuisine.

BASIC RECIPES & TASTY DRESSINGS

Tasty dressings can be used on salads or hot vegetables, or as a sauce to accompany lentil patties, azuki burgers, falafel or plain fish dishes.

TOFU DRESSING

1²/₃ cups / 300 g / 10 oz silken tofu

2 tbs lemon juice

3 tbs oil

pinch of salt

1 tsp soy sauce

1 clove garlic, crushed

Blend all the ingredients together in a liquidiser.

WASTE-NOTHING VEGETABLE STOCK

1–2 tbs oil
2 large onions, chopped
1 clove garlic, chopped
2 carrots, sliced
2 sticks celery, sliced
juice of half a lemon
1 large potato, peeled and diced
½ cup / 100 g / 4 oz lentils, presoaked
cabbage or cauliflower stalks
outer leaves of cabbage, lettuce etc.
any vegetables past their prime, such as soft tomatoes or mushrooms
chopped fresh herbs
8¾ cups / 2 l / 3½ pints water, including any leftover from cooking vegetables, tomato juice drained from cans etc.
salt and freshly ground black pepper
2–3 tbs soy sauce

1 Heat oil in a large saucepan and stir-fry onion and garlic until transparent.

2 Add carrots, celery and lemon juice. Turn the heat to low, cover the pan and sweat, stirring occasionally, for 5–10 minutes.

3 Add remaining vegetables and herbs and pour over the water. Season well and simmer, covered, for about 40 minutes, until vegetables are mushy.

4 Blend the stock and add soy sauce to taste. Keep in the fridge to use within a couple of days or freeze in ice cube trays.

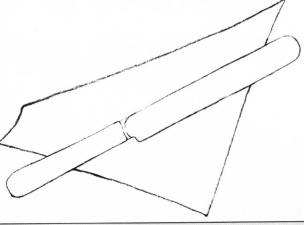

HOT TOMATO SAUCE

1 tbs oil
1 onion, finely chopped
2–3 cloves garlic, finely chopped
1½ cups / 400 g / 15 oz can tomatoes, mashed, with juice
2 tbs tomato purée (paste)
1 tsp ground cumin
1 tsp ground coriander
½ tsp ground chillie
salt

1 Heat oil in a pan, add onion and garlic and stir-fry till soft.

2 Add remaining ingredients, simmer until thickened and check seasoning. Serve with vegetable cous-cous (p 90).

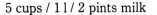

5 cups / 1 l / 2 pints milk

2 tbs unflavoured commercial yoghurt at room temperature

Yoghurt can be made in any sterile container with a tightly fitting lid inside any sort of incubator, such as an oven with the pilot light on or a styrofoam box, but because the secret of successful yoghurt making is a constant lukewarm temperature, it is best to use a special yoghurt maker. Don't put incubating yoghurt near a heat source regulated by a thermostat that switches on and off. Use 2 tbs of the home-made yoghurt to start the next batch. The cost of making yoghurt at home is minimal and the method is easy.

1 Scald the milk. Heat it until it is ready to boil. Just before boiling point, remove the pan from the heat and allow to cool until lukewarm. Test by dripping a little milk on your wrist. It should feel warm, not hot.

2 Put the yoghurt in the chosen container and stir in a little milk until smooth. Now stir in the remaining milk.

3 Cover and place container in the incubator. Be careful not to disturb the yoghurt for about 4 hours. When the consistency is right, chill in the fridge to set before using.

CUCUMBER RAITA

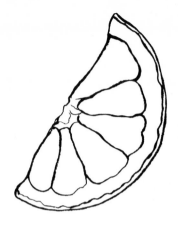

½ cucumber, peeled and chopped
1 small onion, chopped
2 cups / 500 ml / 18 fl oz yoghurt
squeeze of lemon juice
salt and freshly ground black pepper
coriander leaves to garnish

1 Mix all the ingredients together, seasoning to taste, and garnish with the coriander leaves. Use parsley if coriander is not available.

2 Chill well before serving.

Cucumber raita

BLUE CHEESE DRESSING

1 cup / 250 ml / 9 fl oz yoghurt
½ cup / 50 g / 2 oz blue cheese
3 tbs olive oil
salt and freshly ground black pepper

Blend all the ingredients together thoroughly.

Blue cheese dressing

TOMATO DRESSING

4 tbs tomato purée (paste)
3 tbs olive oil
4 tbs lemon juice
2 cloves garlic, crushed
1 small onion, finely chopped
1 tbs honey
pinch of salt

Blend all the ingredients together thoroughly.

TAHINI DRESSING

1 cup / 250 ml / ½ pint tahini

4 tbs water

4 tbs lemon juice

3 cloves garlic, crushed

pinch of salt

Blend all the ingredients together thoroughly.

Tahini dressing

MAYONNAISE

2 egg yolks
½ tsp salt
1 tsp Dijon mustard
1¼ cups / 300 ml / ½ pint olive oil
2 tsp cider vinegar

1 All the ingredients must be at room temperature.

2 Put the egg yolks in a bowl with the salt and mustard and whisk together with a balloon whisk.

3 Beating constantly and evenly, add the olive oil at a very slow trickle. A bottle with a nick cut in the cork can be used to ensure that only a very little oil dribbles out at a time. The aim is to break up the oil into very small globules so that it can be absorbed by the egg yolks. When all the oil has been added you should have a thick glossy emulsion that will cling to the whisk.

4 Gradually beat in the cider vinegar. For a thinner mayonnaise, beat in 1 tbs hot water.

MAYONNAISE MALTAISE

1¼ cups / 300 ml / ½ pint mayonnaise (see above)
grated rind and juice of 2 oranges

Combine the ingredients and serve with cooked vegetables such as asparagus and artichokes, or use as a salad dressing.

Mayonnaise

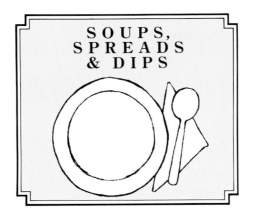

SOUPS, SPREADS & DIPS

CHEESE AND ONION SOUP

Serves 4 – 6

1-2 tbs oil
2 medium onions, sliced
5 cups / 1 1 / 2 pints stock
1½ cups / 250 g / 8 oz potatoes
1½ cups / 175 g / 6 oz Cheddar cheese, grated
salt
soy sauce

1 Heat oil in a large saucepan and stir-fry onions until lightly browned. Add stock and bring to the boil.

2 Meanwhile, peel the potatoes and grate them into the saucepan. Turn down the heat and simmer until potatoes have cooked and soup has thickened.

3 Add the grated cheese, stirring to melt. Season to taste with salt and soy sauce. Serve with wholewheat bread and a crisp green salad.

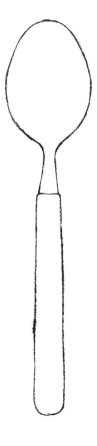

Cheese and onion soup

BEAN SOUP

Serves 4 – 6

1 cup / 250 g / 8 oz field (navy) beans
1-2 tbs oil
1 onion, chopped
1 clove garlic, chopped
2 carrots, chopped
2 stalks celery, sliced
¾ cup / 200 g / 7 oz tomatoes, peeled (or a small can)
1 slice lemon
soy sauce
salt and freshly ground black pepper
parsley

1 Soak the beans overnight. Bring to the boil in a large pan of water (about 5 cups / 1 1 / 2 pints) and simmer until tender.

2 Meanwhile, heat oil in a frying pan and cook onion and garlic until soft. Add carrots, celery and tomatoes, in that order, stirring all the while.

3 Tip vegetables into the pan with the cooked beans. Add the slice of lemon and soy sauce. Taste and adjust seasoning. Heat through and serve sprinkled with chopped parsley. The soup may be partly blended if you like.

Serves 4
knob of butter
1 large onion, chopped
1⅜ cups / 250 g / 8 oz potatoes, peeled
5 cups / 1 1 / 2 pints stock
salt and freshly ground black pepper
3 bunches watercress
To serve:
cream

1 Melt the butter in a large saucepan, add the onion and cook, stirring, until transparent.

2 Add the potatoes, stock and seaoning. Bring to the boil, then simmer until potatoes can be mashed with a fork.

3 Wash watercress and discard tough stalks and yellow leaves. Reserve a few sprigs for garnish, roughly chop the rest and add to the soup. Continue cooking for 2 minutes.

4 Allow the soup to cool slightly, then blend in a liquidizer. Allow to cool completely. Taste and adjust seasoning. Chill and serve with sprigs of watercress to garnish and a swirl of cream.

BORSCHT

Serves 6

2 large onions

3 large beetroot (beets)

3 large carrots

2 parsnips

4 stalks celery

3 tbs tomato paste

4 large tomatoes

½ small white cabbage, shredded

1 tbs honey

1 tbs lemon juice

salt and freshly ground black pepper

handful of chopped parsley

a little untreated (unbleached) white flour

soured cream or yoghurt

1 Cut onions, beetroot (beets), carrots, parsnips and celery into matchsticks. Bring a large pan of salted water to the boil, add the tomato paste and the vegetables and simmer for 30 minutes until tender.

2 Skin the tomatoes, remove the seeds and chop. Add to the pan with the cabbage, honey, lemon juice and seasoning. Simmer for 5 minutes, then throw in a handful of chopped parsley. Check seasoning.

3 If necessary, thicken the soup with a blend of flour and soured cream. The soup is best made the day before it is to be eaten. Reheat and serve with a bowl of soured cream or yoghurt.

GAZPACHO

Serves 4 – 6

500 g / 1 lb large ripe tomatoes
1 large onion
2 cloves garlic
1 green pepper
1 red pepper
½ cucumber
2 slices wholewheat bread
3 tbs olive oil
3 tbs wine vinegar
1¼ cups / 300 ml / ½ pint tomato juice
1¼ cups / 300 ml / ½ pint water
salt and freshly ground black pepper

1 Skin tomatoes, discard seeds and juice and chop the flesh. Peel and finely chop the onion and garlic. Remove pith and seeds from peppers and dice. Peel and dice the cucumber. Cut the crusts from the bread and dice.

2 Put vegetables and bread in a large bowl, pour over the remaining ingredients, stir and season. Chill well — overnight is best for a good tasty soup.

3 You can partly blend the soup if you wish, or blend all of it, in which case offer small bowls of chopped onions, tomatoes, peppers, cucumber and croûtons as a garnish.

HARVEST SOUP

Serves 4 – 6

1-2 tsp oil
1 onion, chopped
2¼ cups / 350 g / 12 oz pumpkin, peeled and diced
2 cups / 250 g / 8 oz carrots, sliced
2 potatoes
juice of half a lemon
5 cups / 1 1 / 2 pints stock
salt and freshly ground black pepper
1 courgette (zucchini), sliced (optional)
⅓ cup / 50 g / 2 oz runner (green) beans, sliced (optional)
basil leaves to garnish

1 Heat oil in a large saucepan and fry onion until translucent.

2 Add pumpkin, carrots and potatoes and pour over lemon juice. Sweat, covered, for 5 minutes.

3 Add stock and seasoning and simmer until potatoes are cooked. Blend or part-blend the soup.

4 If liked, add courgettes (zucchini) and beans and simmer for a further 4 minutes. Check seasoning.

5 Serve garnished with basil leaves. This soup can also be served sprinkled with parmesan cheese.

Harvest soup

D A L

Serves 4

1 cup / 250 g / 8 oz channa dal or yellow split peas
salt
½ tsp turmeric
2 tbs oil or ghee
1 tsp coriander seeds
1 tsp cumin seeds
3 cloves garlic, finely chopped

1 Wash and soak the channa dal (or yellow split peas if dal is unavailable) in plenty of cold water for 4 hours. Drain and wash it once again. Place the dal in a saucepan with 5 cups / 1 1 / 2 pints of water and bring to the boil. Spoon off any scum that forms and add the turmeric. Simmer until tender. Turn the heat down very low as the dal gets mushy and stir to prevent it sticking.

2 Heat the oil or ghee in a pan. When hot, add the seeds and stir. Then add the garlic. Stir-fry until brown. Tip the contents of the pan into the dal and serve hot or cold with Indian bread.

VEGETABLES WITH AIOLI

Aïoli
4 large cloves garlic, peeled
salt and freshly ground black pepper
yolk of 1 egg
¼ cup / 125 ml / ¼ pint olive oil
2 tsps hot water
2 tbs lemon juice

To accompany a selection of raw and cooked seasonal vegetables:

Raw vegetables	Cooked vegetables
carrots	leeks
cauliflower	parsnips
spring (green) onions	courgettes (zucchini)
radishes	green beans
mushrooms	broccoli
capiscums (peppers)	potatoes
tomatoes	artichokes
celery	fennel

1 Pound the garlic into a pulp using a pestle and mortar. Add seasoning.

2 Add the egg yolk and continue pounding until you have a smooth creamy paste.

3 Add the olive oil very gradually, beating well all the time. Don't hurry the process or you'll curdle the sauce.

4 When sauce is thick, mix in the water and lemon juice.

5 Peel and cut up the vegetables into attractive shapes. Steam the vegetables to be cooked until barely tender. Arrange on a large serving platter with the bowl of aîoli in the centre. Serve as a starter.

HUMMUS

Serves 4

1 cup / 250 g / 8 oz chickpeas (garbanzos)	
7½ cups / 1.5 l / 3 pints water	
½ cup / 150 ml / ¼ pint tahina paste	
juice of 2–3 lemons	
3 cloves garlic, crushed	
¼ cup / 75 ml / ⅛ pint olive oil	
salt and freshly ground black pepper	

1 Wash and soak the chickpeas (garbanzos) overnight, then boil in water until tender. Cooking time will vary depending on the age of the peas — anything from 20 minutes to an hour.

2 Purée the chickpeas (garbanzos) in a blender with a little of the cooking liquor and the remaining ingredients. A rough crunchy texture is more interesting than a smooth one. Add more garlic, lemon juice and seasoning to your taste.

3 Serve with a sprinkling of cayenne pepper, a lemon wedge, spring (green) onions, radishes and black olives. Delicious with hot pitta bread (p 107).

SOUPS,
SPREADS
& DIPS

GUACAMOLE

Serves 2-4

2 large ripe avocados
2 large ripe tomatoes
1 bunch spring (green) onions
1–2 tbs olive oil
1–2 tbs lemon juice
salt and freshly ground black pepper
2 green chillies

1 Remove the flesh from the avocados and mash. Skin the tomatoes, remove the seeds and chop finely. Chop the spring (green) onion bulbs.

2 Mix vegetables together with olive oil and lemon juice and season to taste. Garnish with chopped green chillies and serve, chilled, as a dip or with hot pitta bread (see p107).

Far left: Hummus

Left: Guacamole

BROAD (FAVA) BEAN PÂTE

Serves 4
1½ cup / 350 g / 12 oz shelled broad (fava) beans
about 1 cup / 175 g / 6 oz cream cheese
salt and freshly ground black pepper
sprigs of mint

1 If the beans are old, remove the skins before or after cooking. Boil lightly in salted water until tender.

2 Mash or put through a vegetable mill with enough cream cheese to make a thick paste. Season with salt and pepper. Press into individual dishes and garnish each with a sprig of mint. Serve with triangles of wholewheat toast.

SALADS

Potato Salad with Horseradish *38*

Cauliflower, Blue Cheese and Yoghurt Salad *39*

Greek Salad *40*

Spinach and Orange Salad *42*

Kidney Bean, Chickpea (Garbanzo) and Corn Salad *43*

Coleslaw *44*

Strawberry and Avocado Salad *45*

Egg and Pasta Salad *46*

POTATO SALAD WITH HORSERADISH

Serves 4

700 g / 1½ lb new potatoes

⅝ cup / 150 ml / ¼ pint soured cream

3 tbs horseradish, finely grated

pinch of paprika

½ tsp honey

salt and freshly ground black pepper

bunch of spring (green) onions or chives

handful of chopped parsley

1 Wash the potatoes, but do not peel. Boil in salted water until tender.

2 Meanwhile, make the dressing. Combine the soured cream with the horseradish, paprika and honey. Mix well and season with salt and pepper.

3 Trim the spring (green) onions and slit down the stalks so that they curl outwards. Chop the chives.

4 When the potatoes are done, slice them while still hot and mix into the dressing with the parsley. Toss in the onions or chives. Serve immediately, or chill and serve cold.

CAULIFLOWER, BLUE CHEESE AND YOGURT SALAD

Serves 4

1 head of cauliflower

4 tbs yoghurt

2 tbs blue cheese, softened

4 tbs parsley, chopped

salt and freshly ground black pepper

1 Cut the cauliflower into tiny florets — reserve the stalks for use in a soup.

2 Cream the yoghurt and blue cheese together. Toss cauliflower and parsley in the dressing and season well.

GREEK SALAD

Serves 4
1 head crunchy lettuce, shredded
2 Mediterranean tomatoes, sliced
½ cucumber, thinly sliced
1 onion, coarsely chopped
handful of black olives
1½ cup / 175 g / 6 oz feta cheese, cubed
olive oil
salt and plenty of freshly ground black pepper

1 Combine the vegetables and cheese in a large bowl. Pour over enough olive oil to just coat the salad. Season well and toss.

2 Chill for an hour. Toss again, check seasoning and serve.

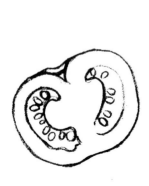

SPINACH AND ORANGE SALAD

Serves 2–4

500 g / 1 lb young spinach leaves
1 bunch watercress
1 large juicy orange
1–2 tbs olive oil
salt and freshly ground black pepper
crispy bacon pieces, optional

1 Use only young tender spinach for this salad. Older leaves are too bitter and tough to be enjoyed raw. Wash the spinach thoroughly, discarding any discoloured leaves and tough stalks. Tear into manageable pieces.

2 Wash the watercress, discarding tough stalks and yellow leaves. Shake water off the spinach and watercress in a lettuce basket.

3 Peel the orange. Remove pith and pips (seeds) and slice as finely as possible. Cut the slices into quarters.

4 Toss the ingredients together in a large bowl with olive oil and season well. Meat eaters can add crispy bacon pieces to this salad.

KIDNEY BEAN, CHICKPEA (GARBANZO) AND CORN SALAD

Serves 4
¾ cup / 175 g / 6 oz kidney beans
¾ cup / 175 g / 6 oz chickpeas (garbanzos)
1 cup / 175 g / 6 oz corn kernels, cooked
6 spring (green) onions
2 very large tomatoes
tofu dressing (see p 10)

1 Soak the kidney beans and the chickpeas separately overnight, then simmer in water until cooked. Drain and cool.

2 Chop the spring onions and slice the tomatoes.

3 Toss all the ingredients in tofu dressing and serve at room temperature with hot pitta bread.

COLESLAW

Serves 6

1 small crisp head of white cabbage

1 cup / 250 g / 8 oz carrots

2 tbs chives, chopped

⅓ cup / 50 g / 2 oz sultanas

1 tbs sesame seeds

mayonnaise (see p 19)

1 Shred the cabbage finely, discarding the stalk. Grate the carrots.

2 Toss all the ingredients together in the mayonnaise and mix well. Taste and adjust seasoning. Chill overnight in the fridge. Mix well again before serving.

Coleslaw

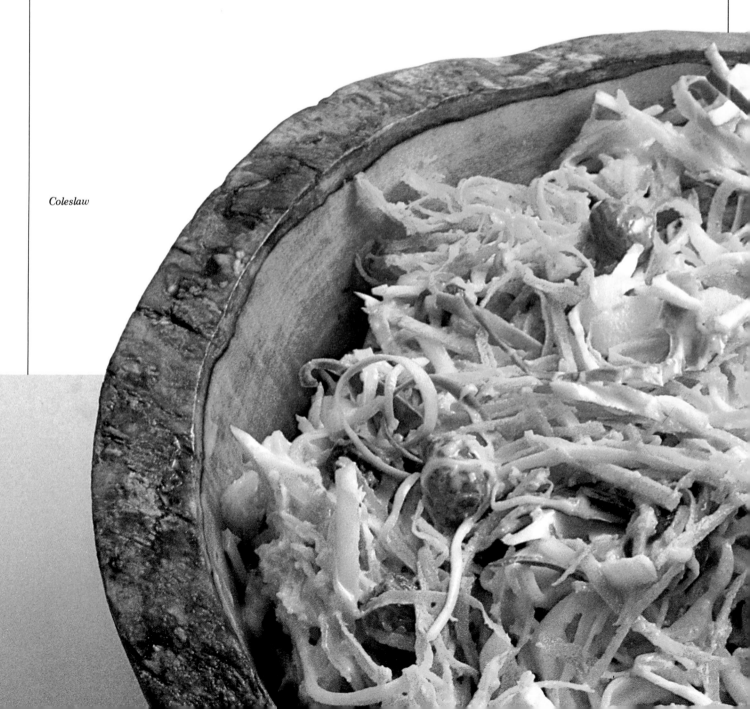

STRAWBERRY AND AVOCADO SALAD

Serves 4

2 avocados
1⅓ cup / 250 g / 8 oz strawberries
2 tbs strawberry vinegar
2 tbs oil
1 tsp honey
salt and freshly ground black pepper

1 Slice the avocados in half, remove the stones and scoop flesh out of shells in one piece if possible, using a palette knife. Slice.

2 Hull and slice the strawberries. Arrange the avocado halves and strawberries on 4 side plates.

3 Mix together the vinegar, oil and honey and season. Pour dressing over salad. Serve as a starter or as an accompaniment to white fish, meat or egg dishes.

EGG AND PASTA SALAD

Serves 4
1 cup / 250 g / 8 oz green or wholewheat pasta shapes
oil
4 eggs
1 cup / 100 g / 4 oz green beans
2 stalks celery
1 dessert apple
½ cup / 50 g / 2 oz walnuts
mayonnaise (see p 19)
salt and freshly ground black pepper
1–2 tbs dill
sliced chicken meat, optional

1 Cook the pasta in plenty of boiling salted water, to which you have added 2 tsp oil, until al dente. Drain and allow to cool.

2 Hard boil (cook) the eggs, peel under cold running water and allow to cool. Cut into quarters.

3 Top and tail the beans and cut into manageable lengths. Simmer in salted water until cooked but not soft. Drain and allow to cool.

4 Chop the celery. Peel, core and dice the apple.

5 Toss all the ingredients except the eggs together in the mayonnaise. Season and garnish with eggs and dill. Meat eaters can add sliced chicken to this dish.

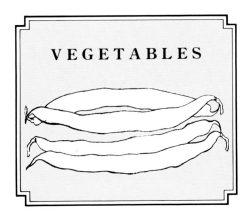

VEGETABLES

BRUSSELS SPROUTS WITH GARLIC AND MUSHROOMS

Serves 4
2–3 tbs oil
4 cloves garlic, chopped
500 g / 1 lb Brussels sprouts, thinly sliced
1¼ cups / 100 g / 4 oz mushrooms, sliced

1 Heat some oil in a wok or deep-sided frying pan. Add the garlic and fry quickly, stirring, until crisp and brown.

2 Add the sprouts and mushrooms and stir until coated with garlic and oil. Stir-fry for 1–2 minutes and eat while crisp and hot. A delicious accompaniment to bean dishes.

VEGETABLES

SPINACH RING

Serves 4
1 k g / 2 lb spinach
6 tbs / 45 g / 3 oz butter
½ cup / 50 g / 2 oz untreated (unbleached) plain flour
1¼ cups / 300 ml / ½ pint milk
⅓ cup / 50 g / 2 oz parmesan cheese
salt and freshly ground black pepper
3 eggs
Tomato sauce
1–2 tbs oil
1 onion, finely chopped
2 cloves garlic, crushed
1½ cups / 400 g / 15 oz can tomatoes, mashed
1 tbs tomato purée
salt and freshly ground black pepper

1 Pre-heat the oven to 190°C / 375°F / Gas 5. Grease a 1.7 l / 7½ cups / 3 pint ring mould.

2 Wash the spinach and discard tough stalks. Pack spinach into a large pan with 2 tbs / 15 g / 1 oz butter and seasoning and cover tightly. Cook over a low heat for about 5 minutes, stirring occasionally, until spinach is soft. Drain and puree in a blender.

3 Now make the cheese sauce. Melt the rest of the butter in a heavy-bottomed pan and add the flour, stirring. Gradually add the milk, stirring continuously. Stir in the cheese and season. Stir until sauce bubbles and thickens, then turn down heat and cook for a further minute. Mix thoroughly with the spinach.

4 Separate the eggs. Beat the yolks into the spinach mixture. Whisk the whites until soft peaks have formed and fold into mixture. Pour mixture into ring mould and bake for 30–40 minutes until risen and lightly set.

5 Meanwhile, make the tomato sauce. Heat the oil in a frying pan and add the onion and garlic. Fry, stirring, until transparent. Add the tomatoes, reserving the juice. Add the tomato paste and season. Simmer for 5 minutes, adding more juice and adjusting seasoning as necessary.

6 To turn out the spinach ring, dip mould into ice-cold water for a few seconds. Run a knife blade round edges of mould. Invert onto a warmed plate. Spoon over the tomato sauce and serve with wholewheat bread or new potatoes and a crunchy salad.

LA LECHUGA

Serves 4

1 tight head of crisp lettuce, Iceberg for preference

4 tbs olive oil

4 cloves garlic, finely chopped

1 Discard looser outer leaves of lettuce. With a very sharp knife, cut lettuce in half from stalk to tip. Cut each half into 3. Keep cold.

2 Heat oil in frying pan and when hot, add garlic. Fry, stirring, until brown. Pour over the lettuce and serve immediately. This is best eaten with the fingers if you don't mind the mess. Offer plenty of paper napkins. Lettuce served this way makes an unusual and appetising start to a summer meal.

SUMMER VEGETABLE PASTIES

Makes 4
Pastry
See page 96
beaten egg to glaze
Filling
1 cup / 100 g / 4 oz potatoes, diced
4 baby carrots, sliced
¼ cup / 50 g / 2 oz garden peas
2 baby courgettes (zucchini), sliced
2 sticks celery, sliced
½ green pepper, diced
Cheese sauce
2 tbs / 25 g / 1 oz butter
4 tbs / 25 g / 1 oz untreated (unbleached) white flour
up to 1¼ cups / 300 ml / ½ pint milk
½ cup / 50 g / 2 oz Cheddar cheese, grated
salt and freshly ground black pepper

1 Make the pastry. Preheat the oven to 180°C / 350°F / Gas 4.

2 Boil the potatoes and carrots in salted water until just tender. In another pan, boil the remaining vegetables for about 2 minutes. Drain.

3 To make the cheese sauce, melt the butter in a heavy-bottomed pan, stir in the flour and gradually add half the milk, stirring. Add the cheese. Stir until melted. Add a little more milk and season to taste. Don't make the sauce too thin or it will pour out of the pastry shells. Mix sauce into vegetables to coat them generously.

4 Divide the pastry into 4 balls and roll out. Share the mixture between the pastry rounds. Crimp together to form pasties and brush with beaten egg. Put the pasties on a baking tray (sheet) and bake in the oven for 30 minutes or until the pastry is cooked.

ARTICHOKES WITH TOMATO SAUCE

Serves 4
4 large artichokes
1–2 tbs oil
1 large onion, chopped
2 cloves garlic, chopped
1½ cups / 400 g / 15 oz can tomatoes, mashed
1 tbs tomato purée (paste)
2 tsps fresh oregano, chopped
lemon juice
salt and freshly ground black pepper

1 Rinse the artichokes thoroughly under the cold tap and leave them upside down to drain. Bring a very large pan of salted water to the boil, put the artichokes in and boil fast for 30–50 minutes, depending on the size. When an outer leaf comes away at a gentle tug, the artichokes are ready.

2 Meanwhile, make the sauce. Heat the oil in a pan and fry the onion and garlic until transparent. Add the tomatoes, tomato purée and oregano and reduce until the sauce is of pouring consistency but not sloppy. Season with salt and pepper and a dash of lemon juice to taste.

3 Drain the artichokes. When cool, pull out the tiny inner leaves together with the hairy inedible choke. Spoon in some tomato sauce. Stand each artichoke in a pool of sauce on an individual dish and serve.

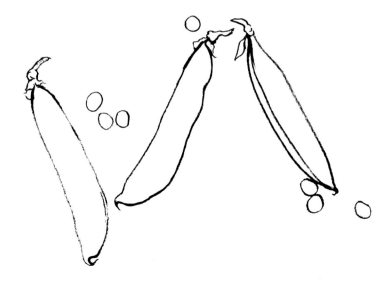

SPICY GREEN BEAN AND TOMATO PASTIES

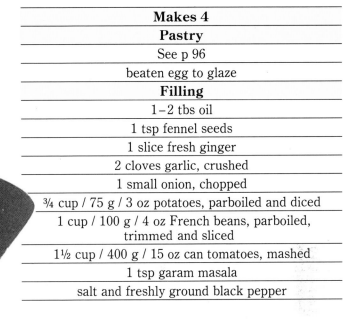

Makes 4
Pastry
See p 96
beaten egg to glaze
Filling
1–2 tbs oil
1 tsp fennel seeds
1 slice fresh ginger
2 cloves garlic, crushed
1 small onion, chopped
¾ cup / 75 g / 3 oz potatoes, parboiled and diced
1 cup / 100 g / 4 oz French beans, parboiled, trimmed and sliced
1½ cup / 400 g / 15 oz can tomatoes, mashed
1 tsp garam masala
salt and freshly ground black pepper

1 Make the pastry and chill for 30 minutes. Preheat the oven to 180°C / 350°F / Gas 4.

2 Heat oil in a pan and when hot, add fennel seeds. Stir in ginger, garlic and onion. Cook, stirring, until lightly browned.

3 Stir in potatoes and beans. Add enough tomatoes and juice to prevent the mixture sticking. Add garam masala, salt and pepper and simmer for about 5 minutes, stirring occasionally and adding more tomato juice as necessary. Do not make the mixture too wet.

4 Divide the pastry into 4 balls and roll out. Share the mixture between the pastry rounds, crimp together to form pasties and brush with beaten egg. Put pasties on a baking tray (sheet) and bake in the oven for 30 minutes or until pastry has cooked. Serve with cucumber raita (p 14).

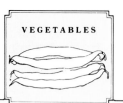

VEGETABLES

GARLIC MUSHROOMS

Serves 4
16 open mushrooms, about 3 cm (1½ inches) across
2 slices wholewheat bread, crumbed
⅝ cup / 150 ml / ¼ pint warm milk
4 cloves garlic
1 cup fresh mixed herbs, chopped
a little oil
salt and freshly ground black pepper
a few sprigs of watercress

1 Preheat the oven to 180°C / 350°F / Gas 4.

2 Wipe the mushroom caps clean. Remove, chop and reserve stalks.

3 Soak the breadcrumbs in milk until soft, then squeeze out excess milk.

4 In a mortar, pound the garlic with herbs and enough oil to make a paste. Pound in the stalks. Mix together with the breadcrumbs and season well with salt and pepper.

5 Spoon the filling into the mushroom caps and arrange them in a lightly oiled ovenproof dish. Bake for about 15 minutes until mushrooms are soft and juicy and filling has crisped a little on the top. Serve hot with sprigs of watercress. Serves 4 as a starter.

STUFFED MARROW OR SQUASH

Serves 4–6

1 marrow or squash
salt and freshly ground black pepper
⅓ cup / 75 g / 3 oz brown rice
2 small carrots, diced
¼ cup / 50 g / 2 oz peas
1-2 tbs oil
1 onion, chopped
1 clove garlic, chopped
1 stalk celery, chopped
1 handful parsley, chopped
2 tbs hazelnuts, chopped
Tomato sauce
1-2 tbs oil
1 onion, chopped
2 cloves garlic, chopped
1½ cups / 400 g / 15 oz can tomatoes, mashed
1 tbs tomato puree (paste)
salt and freshly ground black pepper

1 Pre-heat the oven to 180°C / 350°F / Gas 4. Cut the marrow in half lengthways and scoop out the pith and seeds. Sprinkle the flesh with salt and leave the halves upside down to drain.

2 Meanwhile, make the filling. Simmer the rice in a covered pan of salted water until just tender (about 30 minutes). Drain.

3 Parboil carrots and peas and drain. Heat oil in a pan and fry onion and garlic until translucent. Add celery, carrots and peas. Stir in the rice, parsley and hazelnuts and season well. Dry the marrow and pile filling into one half of it. Top with second half.

5 Make the tomato sauce. Heat oil in a pan and add onion and garlic. Fry, stirring, until soft. Add tomatoes and tomato puree. Simmer for 5 minutes stirring occasionally, and season well.

6 Place marrow in a baking dish with a lid, if you have one big enough, otherwise use foil to cover. Surround it with the sauce. Cover and cook for 45 minutes until marrow is tender. Serve hot or cold with a crisp green salad.

SHREDDED CARROT AND CABBAGE

Serves 4
2 tbs oil
1 tsp mustard seeds
1 tight head of spring greens (greens), finely shredded
500 g / 1 lb carrots, grated
a little honey
salt and freshly ground black pepper

1 Heat oil in a heavy pan with a lid. When it is hot, add the mustard seeds.

2 As soon as the mustard seeds begin to pop, pile in the shredded vegetables, drizzle over the honey and stir well. Turn down the heat, put on the lid and cook for about 3 minutes or until just tender. Season and serve.

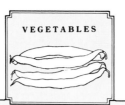

POTATO GNOCCHI

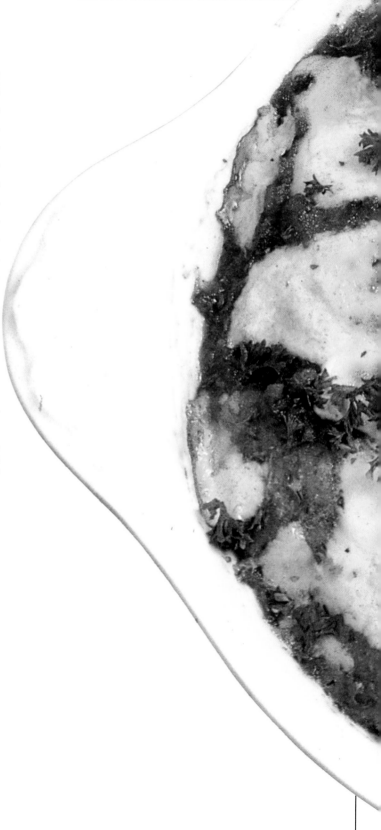

Serves 4
1kg/ 2 lb potatoes
2¼ cups / 250 g / 8 oz wholewheat flour
salt
1 egg
4 tbs / 50 g / 2 oz butter
1 cup / 100 g / 4 oz mozzarella cheese, thinly sliced
Tomato sauce
1–2 tbs oil
1 onion, chopped
2 cloves garlic, chopped
1½ cups / 400 g / 15 oz can tomatoes, mashed
2 tbs tomato purée (paste)
salt and freshly ground black pepper
1 tbs fresh oregano, chopped

1 Preheat the oven to 190°C / 375°F / Gas 5.

2 Peel the potatoes and boil until soft. Mash well. Mash in the flour, salt, egg and half the butter. Shape into balls.

3 Make the tomato sauce. Heat the oil and fry the onion and garlic until soft. Add the tomatoes, tomato purée (paste), seasoning and herbs and simmer, stirring occasionally, for 5 minutes.

4 Layer the gnocchi in an ovenproof dish with the cheese, dotted with butter, and the tomato sauce. Finish with a cheese layer.

5 Bake in the oven for about 20 minutes until the dish has heated through and the cheese has melted.

EGGS

OMELETTE ARCHIE WILLIAMS

Serves 2

½ cup / 100 g / 4 oz smoked cod or haddock

⅝ cup / 150 ml / ¼ pint milk

2 tbs / 15 g / 1 oz butter

4 tbs / 15 g / 1 oz flour

⅓ cup / 40 g / 1½ oz Cheddar cheese, grated

3 eggs

salt and freshly ground black pepper

1 Poach the fish in a little of the milk until cooked. Drain and reserve milk. Skin and flake fish.

2 Melt the butter in a pan and stir in the flour. Gradually stir in the milk, including the milk from the fish, until you have a smooth sauce. Add the cheese and stir until melted.

3 Beat the eggs and season well.

4 Put the fish in a shallow ovenproof dish about 22 cm (8 inches) across. Cover with cheese sauce, then pour over the beaten eggs. Cook under a preheated grill (broiler) set at high for about 7 minutes until the egg is nearly set and the omelette is beginning to brown on top. Serve with salad. This omelette will make a light lunch for 2 people.

EGGS

TORTILLA DE PATATAS

Serves 2–4
2 tbs oil
1 large onion, finely sliced
3 cups / 500 g / 1 lb potatoes, peeled and finely sliced
salt and freshly ground black pepper
4 eggs, beaten

1 Heat the oil in a heavy-bottomed 25 cm (10 inch) frying pan with deep sides. Sauté the onion and potatoes, stirring, for about 5 minutes until lightly browned. Cover and cook gently for 10–15 minutes, until potatoes are tender. Season to taste.

2 Pour over the eggs, pat firmly into a cake and cook, covered, until set. Brown under the grill (broiler) if liked. Allow to cool completely and cut into wedges to serve for a picnic lunch.

TOMATO AND SPINACH LAYERED PANCAKES

Serves 4
Pancake batter
1½ cups / 175 g / 6 oz untreated (unbleached) white flour
pinch of salt
2 eggs
1⅞ cups / 450 ml / ¾ pint milk
1 tbs melted butter
Spinach filling
2 cups / 1 k / 2 lb spinach
2 tbs / 25 g / 1 oz butter
salt and freshly ground black pepper
1⅓ cups / 250 g / 8 oz ricotta
nutmeg to taste
Tomato filling
1 tbs oil
1 large onion, chopped
2 cloves garlic, chopped
1½ cups / 400 g / 15 oz can tomatoes, drained and chopped
1 tbs tomato purée (paste)
2 tsps fresh oregano, chopped
salt and freshly ground black pepper

1 Sift the flour with the salt into a bowl, make a well in the middle, break in the eggs and add the milk slowly, beating to fold in the flour. When half the milk has been added, stir in the melted butter and beat until smooth. Add remaining milk until batter reaches the consistency of thin cream. Leave to stand for at least 30 minutes.

2 For the spinach filling, wash the spinach and discard tough stalks. Melt the butter in a large pot with a tight-fitting lid, add the spinach without shaking it dry and season. Cook, covered, over a very low heat, stirring occasionally, for 8 minutes or until soft.

3 Drain and chop the spinach, then mash it with the ricotta and season with nutmeg. Set aside.

4 For the tomato filling, heat the oil in a pan and fry the onion and garlic until translucent. Add remaining ingredients and heat through, stirring. Add tomato juice if necessary to prevent drying out, but don't allow the mixture to become too sloppy. Set aside.

5 Make the pancakes. Pour a little oil into the pan and when it is hot, spoon in a little batter — enough to coat the bottom of the pan. Tilt and jiggle the pan over the heat until the pancake has formed, then toss or turn it over with a spatula to cook the other side. Discard your first pancake as it will be too oily. Pile the pancakes on a plate as you make them and keep them warm.

6 To assemble the dish, begin with a pancake and spread it with spinach filling. Top this with another pancake and spread with tomato filling. Continue in this way until all your ingredients are used up. Heat the layered pancake through in the oven before serving. This dish can be made in advance and assembled at the last moment before you want to eat.

STILTON OR BLUE CHEESE SOUFFLE

Serves 4
2 tbs / 25 g / 1 oz butter
4 tbs / 25 g / 1 oz untreated (unbleached) white flour
1¼ cups / 300 ml / ½ pint milk
1 cup / 100 g / 4 oz ripe Stilton or blue cheese, crumbled
salt and freshly ground black pepper
4 eggs

1 Preheat the oven to 230°C / 450°F / Gas 8 and grease a soufflé dish.

2 Melt the butter in a small, heavy-bottomed pan and stir in the flour. Gradually add the milk, stirring. When the sauce begins to bubble, turn down the heat and stir for 1–2 minutes until thickened. Remove from the heat and cream in the crumbled cheese. Season. Allow to cool.

3 Separate the eggs and beat the yolks. In a large bowl, whisk the whites with a hand rotary whisk until they form soft peaks.

4 Mix the yolks into the cooled sauce. Stir in 1 tbs of the whites, then lightly fold in the rest and tip into the soufflé dish. Bake for 20–25 minutes or until golden brown and very nearly set. Serve at once with steamed baby courgettes (zucchini).

HERB PANCAKES WITH MUSHROOMS

Serves 6
Pancakes

Add 2 tbs chopped fresh herbs to the batter on page 69 and make the pancakes in the usual way

Filling

6 cups / 500 g / 1 lb mushrooms

milk

salt and freshly ground black pepper

lemon juice

Sauce

4 tbs / 50 g / 2 oz butter

½ cup / 2 oz untreated (unbleached) white flour

1¼ cups / 300 ml / ½ pint milk

½ cup / 50 g / 2 oz Cheddar cheese, grated

1 egg yolk

grated nutmeg to taste

salt and freshly ground black pepper

1 Preheat the oven to 180°C / 350°F / Gas 4. Make the herb pancakes.

2 Wipe, trim and slice the mushrooms. Place in a pan with enough milk to cover, season with salt and pepper and a squeeze of lemon. Poach slowly, stirring occasionally, until mushrooms are soft. Drain and check seasoning.

3 Spoon the filling onto the pancakes, roll up and arrange in a large shallow ovenproof dish.

4 Make the sauce. Melt the butter in a heavy-bottomed pan and stir in the flour. Gradually stir in the milk. When the sauce begins to bubble and thicken, turn down the heat and add the cheese. Stir till melted. Stir in the egg yolk, nutmeg and seasoning.

5 Pour the sauce over the pancakes and bake for about 20 minutes. Serve immediately with salad.

FUL MEDAMES AND EGGS

Serves 4

1 cup / 250 g / 8 oz ful medames
1 tbs oil
1 large onion, chopped
2 cloves garlic, chopped
salt and freshly ground black pepper
4 eggs, hard-boiled (cooked)
parsley

1 Soak the beans overnight. Bring the soaked beans to the boil in fresh water, then simmer till tender (see p 85). Drain and reserve cooking liquor.

2 Heat the oil in a pan and fry the onion and garlic until soft. Blend onion and garlic with enough of the beans and cooking liquor to make a sauce. Season with salt and pepper and mix in with the rest of the beans.

3 Slice the hard-boiled (cooked) eggs on top of the beans and garnish with parsley. Serve with hot pitta bread (see p 107).

Serves 4
6 cloves garlic, chopped
2 tbs olive oil
1½ cups / 250 g / 8 oz shelled prawns or shrimps
4 eggs

1 Fry the garlic in the oil, stirring, until lightly browned.

2 Add the prawns or shrimps and stir-fry until coated with garlic and oil.

3 Divide the mixture between 4 lightly oiled individual serving dishes. Break an egg to one side of each dish. Cover the dishes with foil and cook in a moderate oven for 3–4 minutes until the whites are just set.

PASTA

You will need a large saucepan for cooking pasta, as it tends to stick together if cooked in a small pan with very little water. Add salt and a few drops of oil to the water when it reaches a full rolling boil. Now add the pasta. Fresh pasta will cook in 1–2 minutes. Filled fresh pasta will cook in approximately 8–10 minutes. Dried pasta will take approximately 8 minutes for small shapes, 12 minutes for spaghetti and larger shapes.

PASTA

PASTA WITH AUBERGINE (EGGPLANT) AND APPLE

Serves 2–3

1 large aubergine (eggplant)
1 large cooking apple
1 egg, beaten
seasoned untreated (unbleached) white flour
4 tbs walnut oil
2 cloves garlic, crushed
1 cup / 250 g / 8 oz wholewheat or spinach pasta shapes
salt and freshly ground black pepper

1 Slice the aubergine (eggplant), sprinkle liberally with salt and leave in a colander for 30 minutes. Rinse and dry on kitchen paper and cut into strips. Peel, core and dice the apple.

2 Toss aubergine (eggplant) and apple in the beaten egg, and then in the seasoned flour to give a light coating. Heat some oil in a pan and fry aubergine (eggplant), apple and garlic, stirring, until crisp.

3 Meanwhile, cook pasta shells in plenty of salted water at a full rolling boil, until al dente. Add a few drops of oil to the water to prevent the pasta from sticking. Drain well, season with black pepper and toss in a little walnut oil. Stir in the aubergine (eggplant) mixture and serve with parmesan cheese.

Pasta with aubergine and apple

PESTO

Serves 4

1 cup fresh basil leaves
1 tbs pine kernels
4 fat cloves garlic, chopped
2 tbs parmesan cheese, grated
olive oil
salt and freshly ground black pepper
1½ cups / 350 g / 12 oz spinach twistelli pasta

1 To make the pesto sauce, snip the basil leaves into a mortar. Add the pine kernels, garlic and parmesan cheese. Use freshly grated parmesan for a strong authentic taste.

2 Pound the ingredients together with a pestle, gradually adding enough olive oil to make a thick paste. Season with salt and pepper.

3 Cook twistelli in plenty of boiling salted water with 2 tsp oil added, until al dente. Drain, toss in the pesto and serve with a tomato and onion salad.

PASTA WITH SPINACH SAUCE

Serves 4
1¼ cups / 300 g / 10 oz wholewheat or spinach pasta shapes
1 k g / 2 lb fresh spinach
2 tbs oil
1 onion, chopped
2 cloves garlic, chopped
2⅔ cups / 175 g / 6 oz mushrooms, sliced
1⅓ cups / 250 g / 8 oz quark, ricotta or cream cheese
1–2 tbs pine kernels
salt and freshly ground black pepper
parmesan cheese, grated

1 Wash spinach and discard tough stalks. Pack into a large pan, cover and cook over a low heat until soft, stirring occasionally. Drain and chop.

2 Heat oil in a pan and fry the onions and garlic until soft. Stir in the mushrooms. Cover and cook over a low heat until soft.

3 Mix the vegetables with the cheese and pine kernels and season to taste. Keep warm.

4 Cook the pasta in plenty of boiling salted water until al dente. Drain. Stir sauce into pasta and serve. Offer parmesan cheese.

SPINACH TAGLIATELLE WITH ASPARAGUS

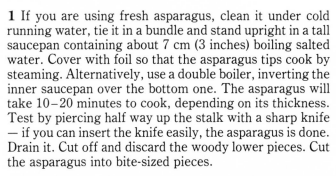

Serves 2 as main course or 4 as a first course
6–7 spears / 250 g / 8 oz asparagus
2 tbs / 15 g / 1 oz butter
4 tbs thin (cereal) cream
salt and freshly ground black pepper
1 cup / 250 g / 8 oz green tagliatelle
2 tsp oil
parmesan cheese, grated

1 If you are using fresh asparagus, clean it under cold running water, tie it in a bundle and stand upright in a tall saucepan containing about 7 cm (3 inches) boiling salted water. Cover with foil so that the asparagus tips cook by steaming. Alternatively, use a double boiler, inverting the inner saucepan over the bottom one. The asparagus will take 10–20 minutes to cook, depending on its thickness. Test by piercing half way up the stalk with a sharp knife — if you can insert the knife easily, the asparagus is done. Drain it. Cut off and discard the woody lower pieces. Cut the asparagus into bite-sized pieces.

2 Melt the butter in a saucepan and toss the asparagus in it. Add half the cream, season and leave for a few minutes over a very low heat to thicken.

3 Meanwhile, cook the pasta until al dente in plenty of boiling salted water to which you have added 2 tsp oil.

4 Drain the pasta, toss in the remaining cream and pour over the asparagus sauce. Serve and offer parmesan cheese.

PASTA WITH MUSHROOM SAUCE

Serves 1 for a luxurious quick lunch
2-4 handfuls green pasta spirals
1 tsp oil
1 cup / 50 g / 2 oz mushrooms
milk
salt and freshly ground black pepper
yolk of 1 egg
1 tbs cream
as much parsley as you like, chopped
parmesan cheese, grated

1 Cook the pasta in plenty of boiling salted water with 1 tsp oil, until al dente.

2 Meanwhile, wipe and slice the mushrooms. Place in a pan with a little milk, season well and poach gently, stirring, until soft and very black and the liquid has almost gone.

3 Beat the egg yolk with the cream and stir in the mushrooms.

4 Drain the pasta and stir in the mushroom mixture with plenty of parsley. Serve at once with parmesan and a tender lettuce salad.

Red lentils

Chickpeas

Brown rice

Azuki beans

Split peas

Cous-cous

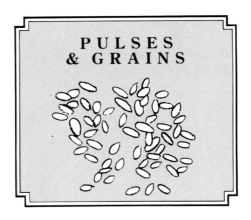

PULSES & GRAINS

Pulses

These are dried seeds such as peas, beans and lentils. They are relatively inexpensive and have a high protein content, which makes them a valuable addition to any diet. In a wholefood or vegetarian diet they may replace meat or fish.

To prepare pulses: pick out any black or discoloured ones and wash under running water. This step can be omitted if using pre-washed brands. The pulses should then be placed in a basin and covered with cold water. Soak overnight before cooking. Tiny red lentils do not need to be soaked before cooking.

To cook: Drain the pulses and cover with plenty of cold water. Do not add salt at this stage or they will remain hard. Bring to the boil and simmer gently until soft. The cooking time will vary according to the age of the pulses and can be anything from 15 minutes to 1½ hours. It is therefore essential to test as the cooking proceeds. As the pulses become tender, add 1 teaspoon of salt for each 1 cup / 250 g / 8 oz and simmer for another 10 to 15 minutes. Drain and use as required. The cooking liquid can be used for making soup or adding to stews.

Note: It is essential to cook red kidney beans for at least 45 minutes before using in salads or any dish which does not have a long cooking time.

Grains

Brown unpolished rice, wild rice or long grain patna rice are ideal for savoury dishes. There are also many 'quick cook' varieties available. To cook these, follow the instructions on the packet.

To prepare rice: allow 3-4 oz per person. Place rice in a fine sieve and hold under the cold tap to wash well. Place in a saucepan with enough cold water to cover the rice 2½ cm / 1 inch above. Add salt.

To cook: bring to the boil and simmer for 15–20 minutes or until all the water has been absorbed. Remove from the heat, cover with a clean cloth (tea towel) and leave for a further 10 minutes. The rice should be fluffy and easily separated with a fork. When using special packets of wild or brown rice, read cooking instructions as these may take longer.

LENTIL AND VEGETABLE PATTIES

Serves 4
1 cup / 250 g / 8 oz lentils
600-900 ml stock
1-1½ pints oil
1 small onion, chopped
1 clove garlic, chopped
½ cup / 50 g / 2 oz potato
¼ cup / 50 g / 2 oz peas
½ tbs fresh thyme leaves
salt and freshly ground black pepper
beaten egg for binding
wholewheat flour for coating
parsley to garnish

1 Soak the lentils for 4 hours and simmer in vegetable stock, or meat stock if preferred, until they can be mashed with a fork. If you use a mild stock, add a little yeast extract to give a sharper taste. Drain the lentils.

2 Heat the oil and fry the onion and garlic until transparent. Boil the potatoes in salted water until cooked, adding the peas just before the end of cooking time. Drain.

3 Put all the vegetables through a mill or mincer. Mix in the thyme and season to taste. Stir in enough egg to make a sticky dough. Form dough into small patties or balls about 3 cm (1½ inches) in diameter.

4 Roll the balls in wholewheat flour and shallow fry in hot oil until crispy on all sides. Garnish with parsley and serve with hot tomato sauce (p 12) and pureed spinach or marrow (squash) in a cheese sauce.

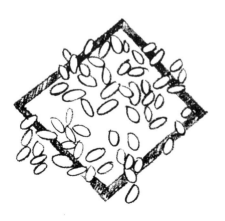

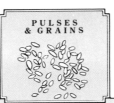

BEAN MOUSSAKA

Serves 4
1 cup / 250 g / 8 oz rose cocoa (pinto or Indian) beans
1 large aubergine (eggplant), thinly sliced
oil
1 large onion, chopped
2 cloves garlic, chopped
1½ cups / 400 g / 15 oz can tomatoes, mashed
1 tbs tomato purée (paste)
2 tsp fresh thyme, chopped
salt and freshly ground black pepper
Cheese sauce
2 tbs / 25 g / 1 oz butter
4 tbs / 25 g / 1 oz flour
1¼ cup / 300 ml / ½ pint milk
½ cup / 50 g / 2 oz Cheddar cheese, grated
grated nutmeg to taste
salt and freshly ground black pepper

1 Soak the beans overnight and cook until you can mash them with a fork (see p 85). Drain.

2 Heat the oven to 180°C / 350°F / Gas 4. Sprinkle the aubergine (eggplant) slices with salt and allow to stand in a colander for 30 minutes. Rinse and pat dry with kitchen paper. Heat some oil in a pan and fry aubergines (eggplant) gently until cooked. Set aside.

3 Add some more oil to the pan and fry the onion and garlic until translucent. Add the tomatoes, tomato purée (paste), thyme and seasoning, and heat through, stirring. Mix in the beans. Set aside.

4 To make the cheese sauce, melt the butter in a thick-bottomed saucepan. Stir in the flour, then gradually add the milk, stirring all the time, until the sauce bubbles and thickens. Turn down the heat, add the cheese and stir till melted. Season with nutmeg and add salt and pepper to taste.

5 To assemble the dish, spread a layer of the bean mixture in the bottom of a casserole and top with aubergine (eggplant) slices. Spread thinly with cheese sauce. Continue to layer the ingredients until they are all used up, ending with a thick layer of the sauce. Bake in the oven to heat right through for 30–40 minutes and serve with a crisp green salad.

PULSES
& GRAINS

KIDNEY BEAN, ARTICHOKE AND MUSHROOM CASSEROLE

Serves 4
1 cup / 250 g / 8 oz kidney beans
1-2 tbs oil
1 large onion, chopped
1–2 cloves garlic, chopped
3 cups / 175 g / 6 oz mushrooms, sliced
1 cup / 100 g / 4 oz French beans, trimmed, cut in thirds and parboiled
1½ cups / 400 g / 15 oz can artichoke hearts, drained
1½ cups / 400 g / 15 oz can tomatoes, mashed
salt and freshly ground black pepper
parsley

1 Soak the kidney beans overnight and cook until tender (see p 85).

2 Preheat the oven to 180°C / 350°F / Gas 4. Heat oil in a pan and fry onion and garlic until translucent. Add the mushrooms and stir-fry for 1–2 minutes until they begin to soften.

3 Transfer all the ingredients to a casserole. Season well. Cover and bake for 30–40 minutes. Sprinkle with parsley and serve with baked potatoes and a green salad.

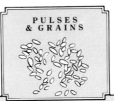

FALAFEL

Serves 4

1 cup / 250 g / 8 oz chickpeas (garbanzos)
3 cloves garlic, minced
1 onion, minced
1 tsp ground cumin
1 tsp ground coriander
2 tbs fresh parsley, finely chopped
1 tbs tahini paste
2 eggs, beaten
lemon juice
wholewheat flour mixed with wheatgerm for coating
oil
olives, gherkins, pickled peppers (optional)

1 Soak the chickpeas (garbanzos) overnight, then cook in boiling water until they can be mashed with a fork.

2 In a large bowl, mash the chickpeas (garbanzos) with the garlic, onion, cumin, coriander, parsley and tahini. Add enough egg and lemon juice to make a dough.

3 Form the dough into 3 cm (1½ inch) balls, roll in flour and wheatgerm to coat and fry in hot oil until crispy. Drain on kitchen paper.

4 Serve hot or cold with a dip of tahini paste mixed with olive oil and lemon juice, and sprinkled with cayenne pepper. Offer olives, gherkins and pickled peppers. Alternatively, stuff the falafel into envelopes of pitta bread with a salad of shredded leaves, peppers and a little chopped chilli.

COUS-COUS

Serves 4 – 6
Cous-Cous
¾ cup–1 cup / 100–175 g / 4–6 oz cous-cous
1 tsp salt
1¼ cups / 300 ml / ½ pint boiling water
3 tbs / 40 g / 1½ oz butter
Vegetable topping
1 tbs oil
2 large onions, chopped
2 leeks, sliced
4 carrots, sliced
5 cups / 1 l / 2 pints stock
salt and freshly ground black pepper
4 courgettes (zucchini), sliced
6 tomatoes, sliced
½ cup / 100 g / 4 oz peas
¾ cup / 100 g / 4 oz kidney beans, presoaked and cooked
¾ cup / 100 g / 4 oz chick peas (garbanzos), presoaked and cooked
a few strands of saffron
Hot tomato sauce
See p 12. Make this in advance.

1 Put the cous-cous in a bowl, add the salt and pour over the boiling water. Let it soak for 20 minutes until the water has been absorbed. Break up any grain that is sticking together.

2 Meanwhile, make the vegetable topping. Heat the oil in a large saucepan and stir-fry the onions and leeks. Add the carrots and stock and season well. Bring to the boil.

3 Place the cous-cous in a vegetable steamer (or a sieve or colander) lined with muslin, and put this over the saucepan. Put on the lid and simmer for 30 minutes.

4 Remove the steamer and add the remaining vegetables and the saffron to the stock. Stir the cous-cous with a fork to break up any lumps. Replace steamer, covered, and continue cooking for 10 minutes.

5 Turn cous-cous into a bowl and stir in the butter. Serve vegetables separately in a tureen. Set the table with soup plates, knives, forks and spoons and offer hot tomato sauce (p 12) and pitta bread (p 107).

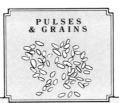

POLENTA

Serves 4 – 6
2¼ cups / 250 g / 8 oz wholewheat flour
⅓ cup / 50 g / 2 oz fine cornmeal
salt and freshly ground black pepper
3¾ cup / 750 ml / 1½ pints water
⅝ cup / 150 g / 5 oz butter
1 cup / 100 g / 4 oz mozzarella cheese, cut into thin strips
To serve:
grated parmesan cheese

1 Place the flour in a bowl and stir in the meal and seasoning.

2 Bring water to the boil and sprinkle in the mixture, stirring with a wooden spoon. Cook over a low heat, stirring occasionally, for about 45 minutes until the mixture is very thick and comes away easily from the sides of the pan.

3 Stir in the cheese. Keep stirring until it melts. Serve hot with Italian tomato sauce (see p 12) and offer parmesan.

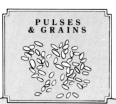

SHRIMP-STUFFED VINE LEAVES

Serves 8
1 packet vine leaves
olive oil
1 large onion, chopped
1 clove garlic, chopped
¼ cup / 50 g / 2 oz green pepper, chopped
¼ cup / 50 g / 2 oz carrot, chopped
¾ cup / 175 g / 6 oz brown rice
2½ cup / 500 ml / 1 pint water or stock
salt and freshly ground black pepper
1½ cups / 250 g / 8 oz peeled shrimps
2 tbs parsley, chopped
soy sauce to taste

1 Preheat the oven to 180°C / 350°C / Gas 4.

2 Heat the oil in a pan and fry the onion and garlic until soft. Stir in the green pepper, carrot and rice. Pour over the water or stock, bring to the boil and season with salt and pepper. Cover and turn the heat down low. Simmer, without stirring, for about 40 minutes.

3 Stir in the shrimps and cook for a further 10 minutes until liquid has been absorbed and rice is tender. Stir in parsley and season with soy sauce to taste.

4 Divide the mixture between the vine leaves and roll up into tight parcels.

5 Pack the vine leaves in an ovenproof dish. Pour olive oil over to coat, cover the dish and cook for 30 minutes until heated through.

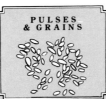
AZUKI BEAN BURGERS

Serves 4

1 cup / 500 g / 8 oz azuki beans
bayleaf
2 onions, chopped
3 cloves garlic, chopped
1–2 tbs oil
4 carrots, peeled and grated
juice of 1 lemon
4 tbs parsley, chopped
salt and freshly ground black pepper
soy sauce to taste
beaten egg for binding
wholewheat flour for coating

1 Soak the azuki beans overnight. Drain, then cook until tender in fresh water with a bayleaf added (see p 85). Drain, reserving the liquid.

2 Fry the onion and garlic in oil until transparent. Add the carrot and lemon juice and sweat, covered, until soft.

3 Add the beans, mix well and puree in a blender, adding a little of the bean liquor if necessary to form a malleable consistency. Stir in the parsley, season and add soy sauce to taste. Stir in enough beaten egg to bind.

4 Form into balls or burgers, coat with flour and shallow fry until brown and crispy on the outside. Serve with a homemade tomato sauce (p 12).

BAKING

1½ cups / 175 g / 6 oz wholewheat flour

pinch of salt

2 tbs sesame seeds

3 tbs oil

2½ cup / 500 ml / ½ pint cold water

1 Combine the dry ingredients with the oil, working it in with your fingers. Slowly add the water to form a dough — you may not need all of it. The dough should be malleable but not sticky.

2 Chill in the fridge before rolling out on a floured surface to use.

WHOLEWHEAT BREAD

4½ cups / 500 g / 1 lb wholewheat flour
2 tbs seeds (sesame, caraway or poppy)
1½ heaped tsp salt
1½ cups / 300 ml / ½ pint warm water
1 tbs / 15 g / 1 oz fresh yeast or 1½ tsp / 7 g / ½ oz dried yeast
½ tsp molasses
1 tbs oil
1 tbs malt extract
beaten egg to glaze
1 tsp seeds (sesame, caraway or poppy) to top the loaf

1 Preheat the oven to 200°C / 400°C / Gas 6. Mix the flour, seeds and salt together in a warm basin (bowl).

2 Pour a little of the water into a small bowl and add the yeast. Put in a warm place for 10 minutes. If using dried yeast, make up according to manufacturer's instructions.

3 Add the oil, the malt extract and the molasses to the rest of the water in a jug.

4 Pour the yeast mixture into the flour and stir. Add enough of the other liquid to make a soft dough, but don't allow it to get too sticky. As different brands of flour absorb different amounts, it may not be necessary to add all this liquid, so don't add it all at once. Gather it with your hands into a ball.

5 Knead the dough for 20 minutes, then place in a greased plastic bag to rise. Put it in a warm place, such as the airing cupboard or a sunny window sill. Leave it there for an hour.

6 Punch down the dough with the heel of the hand to redistribute the raising agent and knead it for a minute. Put it in an oiled loaf tin (pan), 22 × 12 cm (8½ × 4½ inches). Brush the top with beaten egg and sprinkle over the remaining seeds. Cover the loaf with a clean damp tea towel and leave it to rise on top of the stove.

7 Bake for 35 minutes. Turn out of the tin (pan) and flick the bottom of the loaf with your fingernail. It should sound hollow. The sides of the loaf should spring back when pressed. Allow it to cool on a wire rack.

APPLE CAKE

3 medium cooking apples, peeled, cored and sliced
a little cider
1 clove
2 tbs butter, softened
2 tbs honey
2 tbs molasses
1 egg
1 tsp mixed spice
pinch of salt
2 tsp baking powder
1 tsp bicarbonate of soda (baking soda)
½ cup / 75 g / 3 oz raisins
1½ cup / 175 g / 6 oz wholewheat flour
4 tbs / 15 g / 1 oz wheatgerm
1 tsp mixed spice

1 Preheat the oven to 180°C / 350°F / Gas 4.

2 Poach the apple slices in a little cider with the clove until soft. Remove clove. Drain and reserve cider. Purée apples in a blender.

3 In a large bowl mix butter, honey, molasses and 1 tbs of reserved cider. Beat in egg. Stir in apples and remaining ingredients and mix well.

4 Pour batter into a greased and floured loaf tin (pan), 22 × 10 cm (9 × 4 inches), and bake for about an hour until firm. Allow to stand for 10 minutes, then turn out of the tin (pan) and cool completely on a wire rack.

BANANA, NECTARINE AND ALMOND LOAF

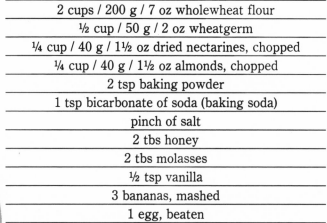

2 cups / 200 g / 7 oz wholewheat flour
½ cup / 50 g / 2 oz wheatgerm
¼ cup / 40 g / 1½ oz dried nectarines, chopped
¼ cup / 40 g / 1½ oz almonds, chopped
2 tsp baking powder
1 tsp bicarbonate of soda (baking soda)
pinch of salt
2 tbs honey
2 tbs molasses
½ tsp vanilla
3 bananas, mashed
1 egg, beaten

1 Preheat oven to 180°C / 350°F / Gas 4.

2 Mix the dry ingredients together in a large bowl. Mix the remaining ingredients together thoroughly in another bowl, then combine the two and stir well.

3 Tip into a greased and floured loaf tin (pan), 22 × 10 cm (9 × 4 inches), and bake for about 50 minutes, or until a toothpick inserted in the middle of the loaf comes out cleanly. Allow to cool for 15 minutes, then tip out of the tin (pan) and cool completely on a wire rack before cutting. Eat it on its own or spread it with butter or cream cheese.

CARROT AND ORANGE CAKE

2 tbs oil
2 tbs honey
2 tbs molasses
2 eggs
2–2½ cups / 250 g / 8 oz carrot, peeled and grated
grated rind of one orange
1 tbs orange juice
2¼ cup / 250 g / 8 oz wholewheat flour
4 tbs / 15 g / 1 oz wheatgerm
1 tsp cinnamon
pinch of salt
2 tsps baking powder
1 tsp bicarbonate of soda (baking soda)

1 Preheat oven to 190°C / 375°F / Gas 5.

2 Beat together the oil, honey, molasses and eggs. Stir in the carrot, orange rind and juice.

3 Combine the dry ingredients in a bowl and stir in the carrot mixture. Mix well. Pour into a greased and floured 22 cm (9 inch) cake tin (pan).

4 Bake for about 30 minutes or until done. Cool for 10 minutes in the tin (pan), then remove and cool completely on a wire rack.

PUMPKIN, SUNFLOWER SEED AND RAISIN CAKE

2¼ cups / 250 g / 12 oz pumpkin

2¼ cups / 250 g / 8 oz wholewheat flour

pinch of salt

2 tsp baking powder

1 tsp bicarbonate of soda (baking soda)

⅓ cup / 50 g / 2 oz sunflower seeds, chopped

⅓ cup / 50 g / 2 oz raisins

2 eggs

2 tbs honey

2 tbs molasses

1 tbs warm water

1 Preheat the oven to 190°C / 375°F / Gas 5. Peel the pumpkin, cut into smallish pieces and boil until tender. Drain and cut up finely.

2 Combine flour, salt, baking powder, sunflower seeds and raisins and mix well.

3 In another bowl, beat the eggs and stir in the honey and molasses. Add 1 tbs of warm water with the pumpkin and beat well.

4 Mix all the ingredients together thoroughly and pour into a greased and floured tin (pan). Bake for 50–60 minutes until done. Allow to stand for 10 minutes in the tin (pan), then cool on a wire rack.

COURGETTE (ZUCCHINI) AND CREAM CHEESE LOAF

4 baby courgettes (zucchini)
1 egg, beaten
4 tbs oil
2 tbs honey
2 tbs molasses
2 tbs cream cheese
1½ cup / 175 g / 6 oz wholewheat flour
½ cup / 50 g / 2 oz soya flour
pinch of salt
2 tsps baking powder
1 tsp bicarbonate of soda (baking soda)

1 Preheat the oven to 170°C / 325°F / Gas 3.

2 Cut the courgettes into thin strips, leaving on the peel, then cut across into 1 cm (½ inch) pieces.

3 Put the egg in a bowl and beat in the oil, honey and molasses. Beat in the cream cheese until smooth.

4 In another bowl, combine the dry ingredients, stirring well. Mix in the courgettes. Gradually stir the dry ingredients into the cream cheese mixture until you have a heavy batter.

5 Transfer batter to a greased and floured loaf tin (pan) and bake for 50–60 minutes until done.

C H A P A T I S

Makes 10

175 g / 6 oz wholewheat flour

6 tbs water

1 Sieve the flour into a bowl. Add the water gradually, drawing the flour together with your fingers to form a dough. Knead until smooth (about 7 minutes). Put dough in a bowl, cover with a damp cloth and leave for 30 minutes.

2 Heat a heavy-bottomed frying pan until very hot (don't put any oil in it). Turn down the heat.

3 Meanwhile, knead the dough for 1 minute, then divide into 10. Roll each portion into a ball on a floured surface, then roll flat with a rolling pin.

4 Lay the chapati in the frying pan and allow it to cook for 8 seconds. Remove it with a spatula and place on a naked flame for 1 second. Turn over the chapati and repeat the process. Cook all the chapatis in the same way, stacking them in a bowl or basket inside a napkin to keep warm.

PITTA BREAD

Makes 8

Follow the wholewheat bread recipe up to the end of
step 5 (page 97)

1 Preheat the oven to 230°C / 450°F / Gas 8.

2 Divide the dough into 8 and roll out into thin ovals.
Place on baking sheets and cover with clean damp cloths.
Leave on top of the stove for 20 minutes.

3 Bake for 5–7 minutes. Allow to cool. These pitta
breads freeze very successfully.

RYE BISCUITS (CRACKERS)

2 tbs / 25 g / 1 oz butter
1 cup / 100 g / 4 oz rye flour
pinch of salt
a little milk, heated

1 Preheat the oven to 180°C / 350°F / Gas 4.

2 Rub the butter into the flour with a pinch of salt, and bind with a little milk to form a dough. Knead for about 7 minutes.

3 Form the dough into about 20 small balls and roll flat on a floured surface.

4 Bake on a biscuit tray (cookie sheet) for about 10 minutes, until the edges are just beginning to brown. Cool on a wire rack. Store in a tin (cookie jar) and serve with butter and cheese.

Rye biscuits

ALMOND BISCUITS (COOKIES)

| 1¼ cups / 175 g / 6 oz ground almonds |
| 1½ cups / 175 g / 6 oz wholewheat flour |
| 2 tbs / 25 g / 1 oz butter |
| 1 tbs oil |
| 1 tbs honey |
| a few drops vanilla essence (extract) |
| halved glacé cherries to decorate |

1 Mix the ground almonds with the flour and work in the butter, oil, honey and vanilla to make a sticky dough. Chill in the fridge.

2 Preheat the oven to 180°C / 350°F / Gas 4. Shape the dough into small biscuits (cookies), decorate each with a cherry and bake for 12 minutes or until golden on a biscuit tray (cookie sheet).

3 Allow to stand for 10 minutes, then cool on a wire rack.

MUESLI BISCUITS (COOKIES)

1 cup / 175 g / 6 oz sultanas or raisins
⅜ cup / 50 g / 2 oz dried apricots, chopped
1 egg, beaten
2 tbs / 25 g / 1 oz butter, melted with 2 tbs hot water
1½ cups / 175 g / 6 oz muesli
1 heaped tbs / 25 g / 1 oz chopped nuts

1 Preheat the oven to 180°C / 350°F / Gas 4.

2 Pick over dried fruit and wash in boiling water. Drain. Put fruit in a bowl and beat well with egg and butter. Stir in museli and nuts.

3 Line a biscuit (baking) tray with greased waxed paper and spread the mixture thinly over it. Mark into fingers and bake for 45 minutes.

4 Cut fingers through and allow to cool for 10 minutes before removing from the tray. Finish cooling on a wire rack.

DESSERTS

FRESH FRUIT DESSERT CAKE

Serves 8
2 eggs
¼ cup / 75 ml / ⅛ pint milk
2 tbs honey
2 tbs molasses
1½ cup / 175 g / 6 oz wholewheat flour
1 tsp baking powder
1 tsp bicarbonate of soda
1 tsp cinnamon
pinch of salt
500 g / 1 lb peaches
250 g / ½ lb plums
250 g / ½ lb cherries
1 cup / 100 g / 4 oz walnuts, chopped
a little butter
fresh fruit to decorate
To serve:
whipped cream

1 Preheat oven to 200°C / 400°C / Gas 6.

2 Beat the eggs with the milk. Stir in the honey and molasses. Stir in the rest of the dry ingredients and mix well.

3 Stone and chop the fruit. Mix it into the batter with the nuts. Pour into a greased and floured 22 cm (9 inch) cake tin with a removable bottom (spring form cake pan) and bake for 50–60 minutes until set in the middle. Dot with butter towards the end of the cooking time to prevent the top drying out.

4 Allow to cool in the tin (pan). Chill in the fridge, decorate with fresh fruit and serve with whipped cream.

PECAN PIE

Serves 4 – 6
1½ cup / 250 g / 8 oz pastry (see page 96)
4 tbs / 50 g / 1 oz butter, softened
2 tbs honey
2 tbs maple syrup
3 eggs
1 tsp vanilla essence (extract)
1 cup / 100 g / 4 oz pecan halves
To serve:
whipped cream

1 Preheat the oven to 220°C / 425°F / Gas 7. Line a 22 cm / 8½ inch pie dish (plate) with pastry. Prick and bake blind for 10 minutes.

2 Meanwhile, make the filling. Beat the butter together with the honey and syrup until smooth. In another bowl, beat the eggs and vanilla essence thoroughly with a wire or rotary whisk. Pour in the syrup, beating constantly with a fork.

3 Scatter the nuts evenly over the pastry base (shell) and pour the custard over. Bake in the middle of the oven for 10 minutes. Reduce the heat to 160°C / 325°F / Gas 3 and bake for a further 25 – 35 minutes until the filling is set, but not dry.

4 Serve warm (but not hot) or cold with whipped cream.

Pecan pie

SWEET POTATO AND APRICOT PANCAKES

Serves 6 – 8
Pancakes
See p 68
Filling
¾ cup / 100 g / 4 oz dried apricots

2 large sweet potatoes

butter

honey

cinnamon

soured cream

1 Soak the apricots overnight. Bring to the boil and simmer till tender. Drain and reserve the liquid. Chop the apricots.

2 Peel and roughly cut up the sweet potatoes. Put in a saucepan, pour over the apricot liquid and cover with water. Bring to the boil and simmer until cooked.

3 Mash the sweet potatoes with a little butter. Add honey and cinnamon to flavour. Mix in the apricots.

4 Place a dollop of mixture onto each pancake and roll up. Heat through and serve with a drizzle of honey and soured cream.

RICH HONEY AND PLUM ICE CREAM

Serves 4

1 cup plums
1 tbs milk powder
6 tbs honey
2 tbs yoghurt
a few drops vanilla essence (extract)
⅝ cup / 150 ml / ¼ pint thick (whipping) cream

1 Put plums in a bowl and pour over boiling water. After 1 minute, the skins will split. Drain and pour over cold water. Peel the fruit, discard the stones and chop finely.

2 Purée the fruit with the milk powder and honey in a blender until smooth. Stir in the yoghurt and vanilla essence (extract). Freeze the mixture.

3 When the mixture is almost frozen, remove it from the freezer and beat it. Whisk the cream and stir the two together. Return to the freezer.

APPLE AND AZUKI BEAN PIE

Serves 4 – 6

Pastry

See p 96

beaten egg to glaze

Filling

1 cup / 250 g / 8 oz azuki beans, presoaked and cooked

2 cooking apples, peeled, cored and sliced

2 tbs honey

1 tsp mixed spice

beaten egg to glaze

To serve:

cream

1 Preheat the oven to 230°C / 450°F / Gas 8. Make the pastry and chill in the fridge. Cut the chilled pastry in half, roll it out and line a greased 22 cm (8 inch) pie dish (plate).

2 Mix the azuki beans with the apples, honey and spice and fill the pie. Cover with remaining pastry, glaze with beaten egg, make a slit in the top and bake for 30 – 40 minutes until golden brown. Serve with cream.

APPLE, STRAWBERRY AND BLACKBERRY CRUMBLE

Serves 4
4 cooking apples
1 tbs honey
⅔ cup / 100 g / 4 oz strawberries
¾ cup / 100 g / 4 oz blackberries
2¼ cup / 250 g / 8 oz wholewheat flour
½ cup / 100 g / 4 oz butter
2 tbs sesame seeds
1 tsp mixed spice
pinch of salt
To serve:
cream

1 Preheat the oven to 180°C / 350°F / Gas 4.

2 Peel and core the apples and cut into slices. Put apples in a shallow ovenproof dish with a little water and the honey and cook, covered, in the oven for 30 minutes.

3 Meanwhile, hull and slice the strawberries and pick over the blackberries.

4 Now make the crumble. Place the remaining ingredients in a bowl and rub in the butter with the fingers until the mixture resembles fine breadcrumbs.

5 When the apples are ready, mix in the strawberries and blackberries, adding a little more honey if liked. Press the crumble mixture gently on top of the fruit and return to the oven for 15 minutes until golden brown. Serve hot or cold with cream.

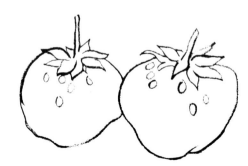

BROWN RICE PUDDING

Serves 4
½ cup / 100 g / 4 oz brown rice
2½ cups / 500 ml / 1 pint China tea
1 stick cinnamon
⅓ cup / 50 g / 2 oz sultanas
⅜ cup / 50 g / 2 oz dried apricots, chopped
¼ cup / 50 g / 2 oz almonds
To garnish:
sliced fresh fruit

1 Wash the rice thoroughly under running water. Put it in a heavy pan with the tea and simmer gently for about an hour with the cinnamon.

2 Preheat the oven to 180°C / 350°F / Gas 4. Remove the cinnamon and transfer the rice to an ovenproof dish. Stir in the remaining ingredients and bake for about 25 minutes until done. Serve hot or refrigerate and serve cold. Garnish with sliced fresh fruit, if liked.

COEUR A LA CREME

Serves 4
1⅓ cups / 250 g / 8 oz cream cheese
½ cup / 100 g / 4 oz yoghurt
1⅓ cups / 250 g / 8 oz strawberries
⅝ cup / 150 ml / ¼ pint cream
1–2 tbs honey

1 Blend the cream cheese with the yogurt and pack into the small heart-shaped moulds traditional with this dessert. Chill.

2 Make a strawberry sauce by blending half the strawberries with the cream and honey. Unmould the cheeses onto individual plates, surround with the sauce and decorate with the remaining strawberries.

PEARS WITH STILTON OR BLUE CHEESE & WALNUT STUFFING

Serves 4 – 8

2 large or 4 small ripe pears

1½ cup / 175 g / 6 oz Stilton or blue cheese

½ cup / 50 g / 2 oz walnuts, chopped

1 Wash the pears, remove the stalks, cut in half and carefully remove the cores.

2 Crumble the cheese and mix it with the chopped walnuts. Pile the mixture into the pear halves and serve.

HONEY AND LEMON CHEESECAKE

Serves 4 – 6
Biscuit (crumb) crust
100 g / 4 oz / wholewheat biscuits (crackers)
1 tbs ground almonds
4 tbs / 50 g / 2 oz butter
Filling
2 eggs
4 tbs honey
2 cups / 350 g / 12 oz full fat cream cheese
juice and rind of half a lemon

1 Preheat the oven to 180°C / 350°F / Gas 4.

2 Place biscuits in a plastic bag and pound with a hammer until biscuits crumble. Melt butter and stir into biscuit crumbs and ground almonds. Grease an 18 cm (7 inch) loose-bottomed flan tin (pie plate) and press biscuit mixture evenly into base.

3 Separate the eggs. Beat the yolks with the honey, then beat in the cream cheese. Stir in the lemon rind and juice and beat until smooth.

4 Whisk the egg whites until they form soft peaks and fold into the cheese mixture. Pour over the biscuit mixture and smooth the surface.

5 Bake in the middle of the oven for about 20 minutes until set and just turning golden. Cool in the tin (pie plate). Remove sides of tin (pie plate) and chill in the fridge before serving.

INDEX

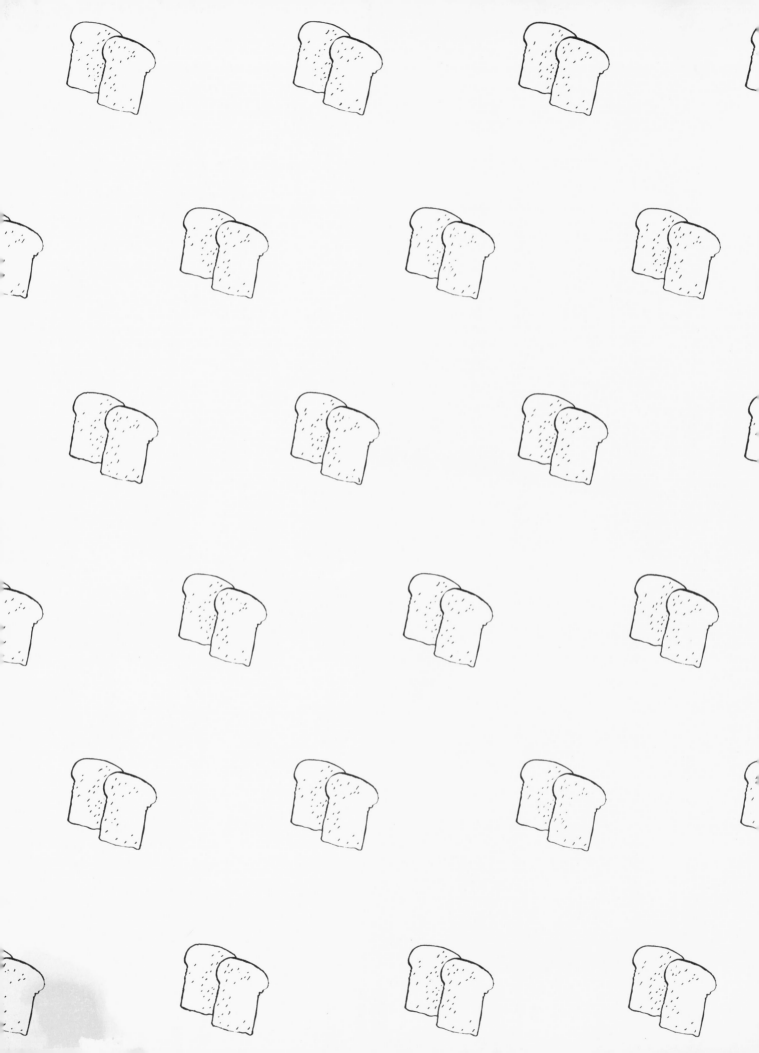